Kind Ninja

ACTIVITY BOOK

T0060092

Ninja Life Hacks®

Welcome

Hey there, ninjas! My name is Kind Ninja. My book is packed with everything from fill-in fun to puzzles and games.

This book belongs to

.....

.....

Are you ready to come and meet my friends?

KINDNESS ROCKS!

If you're looking for ways to spread kindness, then this is the book for you! From kindness mantras to quizzes, mindfulness techniques, and cool challenges, there are so many things you can do! This book is also packed with ways to be kind to yourself—that's just as important, remember!

Contents

Ninja Life Hacks®

PAGES 4-9 ..... HELLO WORLD!
PAGE 10 ..... WHAT COMES NEXT?
PAGE 11 ..... MATCH UP
PAGE 12 ..... I AM FEELING . . .
PAGE 13 ..... KINDNESS MANTRA
PAGES 14-15 ..... TWIST OF KINDNESS
PAGES 16 ..... MY KIND OF TREAT
PAGES 17 ..... HOLD HANDS
PAGES 18-19 ..... SPREAD KINDNESS
PAGE 20 ..... WORD SEARCH
PAGE 21 ..... BOUQUET OF KINDNESS
PAGES 22-23 ..... EVERYONE IS WELCOME
PAGES 24-25 ..... SELF-CARE
PAGES 26-27 ..... SPOT THE DIFFERENCE
PAGE 28 ..... SHARING IS CARING
PAGE 29 ..... MIX UP
PAGES 30-31 ..... THE ROAD TO KINDNESS
PAGE 32 ..... YOU CAN DO IT!
PAGE 33 ..... SIZE SORTING
PAGES 34-35 ..... STICK TOGETHER
PAGE 36 ..... SUDOKU
PAGE 37 ..... LEAN ON ME
PAGE 38 ..... TO THE PARK
PAGE 39 ..... WHICH NINJA?
PAGES 40-41 ..... KINDNESS AT PLAY
PAGE 42 ..... YOU'VE GOT THIS
PAGE 43 ..... CRACK THE CODE
PAGES 44-45 ..... WHAT CARING JOB SHOULD I DO?
PAGE 46 ..... COLOR ME KIND
PAGE 47 ..... ALL SCRAMBLED UP!
PAGES 48-49 ..... LET'S SKETCH
PAGES 50-51 ..... A GOOD FRIEND IS...
PAGE 52 ..... CHEERFUL MESSAGE
PAGE 53 ..... MY KINDNESS PLEDGE
PAGES 54-55 ..... BE KIND
PAGE 56 ..... LOST LUNCH
PAGE 57 ..... SPREAD THE WORD
PAGE 58 ..... KINDNESS BANQUET
PAGE 59 ..... LET'S SKATE
PAGE 60 ..... CELEBRATE DIFFERENCE
PAGE 61 ..... SHOW SUPPORT
PAGES 62-63 ..... ACTS OF KINDNESS
PAGE 64 ..... MIX UP
PAGE 65 ..... COME TOGETHER
PAGES 66-67 ..... WHAT KIND OF FRIEND ARE YOU?
PAGE 68 ..... SHOW COMPASSION
PAGE 69 ..... MAKE A KINDNESS FLOWER
PAGES 70-71 ..... 30-DAY KINDNESS CHALLENGE
PAGES 72-73 ..... FOUR WAYS
PAGE 74 ..... LET'S PLAY SQUARES
PAGE 75 ..... TAKE THE TROPHY
PAGES 76-77 ..... KINDNESS COUNTS
PAGE 78 ..... KIND WORDS
PAGE 79 ..... BE INCLUSIVE
PAGE 80 ..... ANSWERS

HELLO WORLD!

Grab your pens and pencils. It's time to fill in these pages with all the things that matter to you!

My name is .....

My friends call me .....

I am ..... years old

I live in .....

I live with .....

.....

.....

.....

My kindest friend is

.....

My kindest family member is

.....

When somebody is kind to me, I feel:

- ☐ Happy
- ☐ Loved
- ☐ Joyful
- ☐ Calm
- ☐ Content
- ☐ .....
- ☐ .....

My favorite colors are . . .

Color them in!

Do something kind for someone you love! Perhaps you could make them a card, give them flowers, or give them a big hug. Draw or write about what you are going to do here.

Ninja Life Hacks®

Treat yourself

Being kind to yourself is important. Choose how you would spend your perfect day. Check as many of these hearts as you want.

- Beach day ☐
- Bike riding ☐
- Reading ☐
- Baking ☐
- Playing sports ☐
- Listening to tunes ☐
- Drawing or painting ☐
- Crafting or making things ☐
- Watching movies ☐
- Swimming ☐
- TV marathon ☐
- Nature walk ☐
- Being with friends ☐

Unkind things

Circle the ways that you have seen people being unkind. Can you think of any other examples?

Criticizing clothes

Saying mean things

Making fun of others

Not inviting someone to a party

Leaving someone out

Ignoring someone

.....

.....

.....

Kind things

Now circle the ways that you have seen people show kindness. Can you think of any other examples?

Inviting someone to join in

Sharing a snack

Saying something encouraging

Opening a door

Helping others with homework

Comforting someone

.....

.....

.....

MY FAVORITE THINGS

Fill in one answer for each category.

Music: .....

TV show: .....

Movie: .....

Food: .....

Candy bar: .....

Place: .....

Flower: .....

Color: .....

Subject at school: .....

Animal: .....

THIS OR THAT

Circle which option you prefer for each one.

SWEET OR SOUR

FALL OR SPRING

LOUD OR QUIET

HOT OR COLD

SUNSHINE OR SNOW

SHOWER OR BATH

DRAMA OR COMEDY

ONE BEST FRIEND OR LOTS OF FRIENDS

WHY I LOVE BEING KIND

Check the boxes to choose from the options below, and then write your own ideas!

- ☐ I like making people happy
- ☐ It makes me feel good
- ☐ It's fun
- ☐ That's what friends are for
- ☐ _____
- ☐ _____
- ☐ _____
- ☐ _____
- ☐ _____

WHAT WAS THE LAST KIND THING YOU DID? WRITE OR DRAW ABOUT IT IN THIS SPACE.

WHAT COMES NEXT?

Kind Ninja has a feel-good challenge just for you! Circle the correct picture at the end of each row to show what comes next in the sequence.

A

B

C

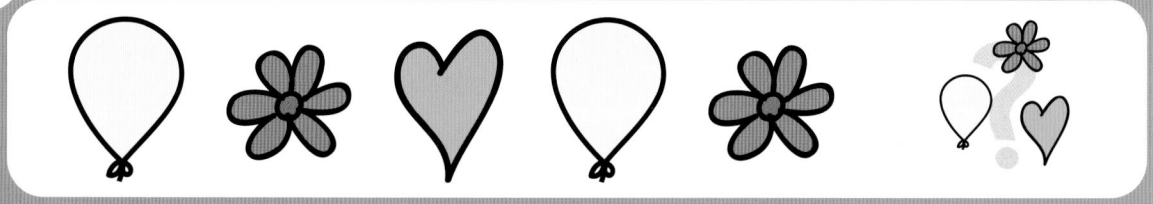

D

MATCH UP

Look carefully at the pictures of Kind Ninja on this page. Which two match each other exactly? Draw circles around the matching pair, then color them in.

I AM FEELING . . .

Take a moment to think about how you feel today. Look at the emotions below and see which one sounds like you, then draw a circle around it.

Tired

Stressed

Sad

Happy

Calm

Energetic

Excited

Shy

Bored

Peaceful

Confident

NOW COLOR IN A SELF-CARE IDEA TO TRY.

Breathe in and out slowly five times.

Remember a task you tried your best to do.

Think of something that went well today.

Draw a picture of your favorite place.

Remember a time you made someone laugh.

KINDNESS MANTRA

Use the space below to write your own kind mantra. It can help you through anything life throws at you! Repeat your mantra each day to give yourself a boost.

HERE ARE SOME IDEAS FOR INSPIRATION!

I am kind.
I am strong.
There is nobody quite like me.
Making mistakes is okay.
I can do this.
I have a voice.
I will be heard.

How did this activity make YOU feel?

Add a thumbs up or a thumbs down sticker here.

TWIST OF KINDNESS

Everyone feels negative about themselves at some point, but there are ways you can train your brain into being kinder. See if you can rewrite these phrases to turn them into positives!

I did the first one for you to show you how it works!

I did badly on my spelling test.

I will practice my spelling before my next test.

I get nervous when I read out loud in class.

Everyone is better than me.

I am terrible at math.

I can't do it.

I always get things wrong.

I'm not as confident as my friends.

I want to give up.

I will never be able to do that.

What's the point in trying?

I'm Positive Ninja. It's amazing how some positive thinking can change the way you feel about yourself.

MY KIND OF TREAT
Kind Ninja wants to treat Angry Ninja to an ice cream cone. Can you find the ice cream that matches this one exactly?
No other ice cream will do!

HOLD HANDS

Remember that a kind little gesture, like holding someone's hand, can make a big difference! Decorate this picture with heart and flower stickers, then use your favorite colors to finish it.

SPREAD KINDNESS
Kind Ninja is on a mission and needs your help! Use your finger or a pencil to travel through the maze, delivering presents to each friend. Add a present sticker next to each ninja you meet.
I want to give one present to each friend.
START
Wow, thank you!
This is awesome!

This present is amazing!
Thank you!
I'm so grateful!
FINISH

WORD SEARCH

How many words about kindness can you find in this word search? Ready, set . . . go!

CHECK OFF EACH WORD WHEN YOU FIND IT IN THE GRID!

A	T	H	O	U	G	H	T	F	U	L	R	U	Y	F
G	U	A	C	O	Y	H	O	P	I	Q	Z	F	N	K
P	A	R	F	C	P	N	R	C	X	Z	O	B	K	J
A	E	N	F	A	C	L	U	O	M	Y	M	P	I	D
T	W	D	Q	R	O	E	U	M	S	A	H	F	N	A
I	S	Z	U	I	I	E	X	P	O	H	E	S	D	E
E	Y	P	P	N	A	H	G	A	B	N	L	A	O	F
N	H	G	C	G	C	E	P	S	T	Q	P	Y	H	V
C	F	C	E	X	D	M	U	S	H	L	F	B	G	Y
E	T	I	L	N	X	N	L	I	S	E	U	B	D	I
A	X	O	E	A	T	Y	I	O	H	T	L	K	Y	Z
R	H	U	G	T	X	L	H	N	Q	K	C	M	S	Q
O	T	Z	V	L	O	V	E	B	T	I	O	N	F	U
S	E	L	F	N	E	S	S	S	C	C	M	K	B	L
E	A	M	N	I	D	L	R	Y	E	Q	Y	S	N	M

- ☐ THOUGHTFUL
- ☐ CARING
- ☐ KIND
- ☐ SELFLESS
- ☐ COMPASSION
- ☐ LOVE
- ☐ GENTLE
- ☐ HUG
- ☐ PATIENCE
- ☐ HELPFUL

BOUQUET OF KINDNESS

Get creative and draw a bouquet of lots of colorful flowers. They can be any kind you like! Who would you give it to?

How did this activity make YOU feel?

Add a thumbs up or a thumbs down sticker here.

I'm Creative Ninja, and I love drawing beautiful things!

EVERYONE IS WELCOME

Kind Ninja knows how important it is to include everybody. The more kindness you share with others, the better! Check out these ways to be more caring to those around you.

BE FAIR!
ALWAYS TREAT OTHERS FAIRLY AND WITH RESPECT. MAKE SURE EVERYONE IS LISTENED TO AND SUPPORT ONE ANOTHER!

ACCEPT DIFFERENCES
THERE ARE MANY WAYS OTHERS MAY BE DIFFERENT FROM YOU . . . THE WAY THEY LOOK OR DRESS, WHAT THEY BELIEVE IN, WHERE THEY LIVE, OR WHAT THEY ENJOY DOING!

Can you think of a time when you were treated unfairly? Write about how it made you feel here.

.....

.....

.....

Write down three ways you are different from your best friend.

1. .....

2. .....

3. .....

INCLUDE EVERYBODY

If I notice someone playing on their own, I will . . .

GRAB A PEN OR PENCIL AND WRITE DOWN SOME WAYS YOU CAN TREAT OTHERS WITH KINDNESS!

ALWAYS BE KIND

When someone is upset, I will . . .

If my friend is struggling with their work, I will . . .

SELF-CARE

Do you ever take time out to take care of yourself? Self-care is all about the little things you can do to be kind to yourself. Go on, treat yourself!

What do YOU need today?

WHY NOT TRY OUT SOME OF KIND NINJA'S IDEAS? COLOR IN EACH ONE WHEN YOU TRY IT!

Take a bubble bath	READ A BOOK	Dance like nobody is watching	Say something that you love about yourself out loud every day
DO SOME STRETCHES	Draw, paint, or make something	Watch your favorite TV show	TRY SOME RELAXING BREATHING
Keep a scrapbook of things you love	GO OUTSIDE AND ENJOY NATURE	Look through some old photos	CURL UP IN A WARM BLANKET

Listen to your favorite song	Take time to organize your room	List 5 things you are grateful for	PLAY A BOARD GAME
BAKE SOMETHING			

CAN YOU THINK OF ANY MORE? WRITE YOUR OWN IDEAS IN THE EMPTY SPACES.

How did this activity make YOU feel?

Add a thumbs up or a thumbs down sticker here.

SPOT THE DIFFERENCE

Having a hobby that you love is the perfect way to practice self-care. Can you spot eight differences between these pictures of Kind Ninja and Positive Ninja having fun at their karate class?

Add a star sticker or color in a circle below for every difference you spot.

SHARING IS CARING

Kind Ninja brought donuts to school for everyone to enjoy. Draw lines to pass out the donuts so that each ninja has the same number. How many donuts will each one get?

MIX UP

Shy Ninja was sitting alone at lunch, but an invitation from Kind Ninja soon solved that problem! Can you put the jumbled-up picture back together?

Write the letters in the correct order here.

THE ROAD TO KINDNESS
Like Kind Ninja, Caring Ninja knows it feels good to help other people whenever you can. Follow the trail and help each ninja when you meet them along the way.
START
Lonely Ninja
Color in the umbrella to shelter Lonely Ninja from the rain.
Hardworking Ninja
Draw a broom to sweep up leaves.
Worry Ninja
Those bags look heavy! Cross out half of the bags to share the load.

Circle the item needed to wash the dishes.
Disappointed Ninja
Nervous Ninja
Nervous Ninja is worried about going to a party. Write something that you could say or do to help.
I'm Caring Ninja. Kindness is about looking out for others.
Caring Ninja

YOU CAN DO IT!
Fill in the letters using your favorite colors, then try to remember this message wherever you go!
SPREAD
COLOR IN KIND NINJA AND THIS MANTRA TO COMPLETE THIS POSTER!
KINDNESS

SIZE SORTING
Frustrated Ninja is struggling with a sorting task. Can you help out by sorting these items into size order, from smallest to biggest?
GIVE EACH ITEM A NUMBER FROM 1 TO 10. MAKE 1 THE SMALLEST AND 10 THE BIGGEST.
A
B
C
D
E
F
G
H
I
J
STOP
WHEN THINGS GETS FRUSTRATING, FRUSTRATED NINJA TAKES A DEEP BREATH AND COUNTS TO 10. GIVE IT A TRY—IT COULD BE YOUR NEW SECRET WEAPON!
I'm going to give up!
Don't give up—we'll do it together!

STICK TOGETHER

Lonely Ninja is feeling down in the dumps, so some of the other ninjas have arrived to bring some cheer! Connect the dots to surround Lonely Ninja with awesome friends!

Zen Ninja
Creative Ninja
Lazy Ninja
I feel so much better now. Thank you for your kindness!
That's what friends are for!
How did this activity make YOU feel?
Add a thumbs up or a thumbs down sticker here.

SUDOKU

Puzzles are lots of fun, and completing one can make you feel great! Try this sudoku challenge from Problem-Solving Ninja! There should only be one of each tool in every row, column, and small square.

LEAN ON ME

Nervous Ninja is worried about school. What could you do to help? Look at the ideas below. Put a heart-shaped flower sticker next to the ones you would try, then cross out any you think wouldn't work.

Listen to Nervous Ninja's worries

Tell Nervous Ninja a joke

Tell them what you ate for dinner

Give them a hug

Make fun of them

Tell them about a time you overcame your own nervousness

Tell them what you love about them

WHAT ELSE DO YOU THINK WOULD COMFORT A FRIEND IN THIS SITUATION? WRITE SOME OF YOUR OWN IDEAS IN THE BLANK CLOUDS.

TO THE PARK

Forgetful Ninja can't remember the way to the park. Can you show some kindness by helping this ninja through the tricky maze?

WHICH NINJA?

Kindness is all about helping out. Read each problem below, then pick a ninja who can help. Draw lines to match each problem to the ninja that's perfect for the job!

I don't feel like doing anything.

I'm feeling sad.

I need to learn my times tables!

I can't concentrate!

I want someone to come on an adventure!

Focused Ninja

Curious Ninja

Memory Ninja

Motivated Ninja

Caring Ninja

KINDNESS AT PLAY

Kindness means including everybody! The ninjas on the playground have a challenge for you. How many of each item can you spot in the big picture? Write your answers in the boxes.

YOU'VE GOT THIS
Small acts of kindness can make a big difference in someone else's day. Color in the picture of Kind Ninja helping to carry the groceries.

CRACK THE CODE

Can you decode this caring message? Each symbol represents a letter. Use the key to help you crack the code!

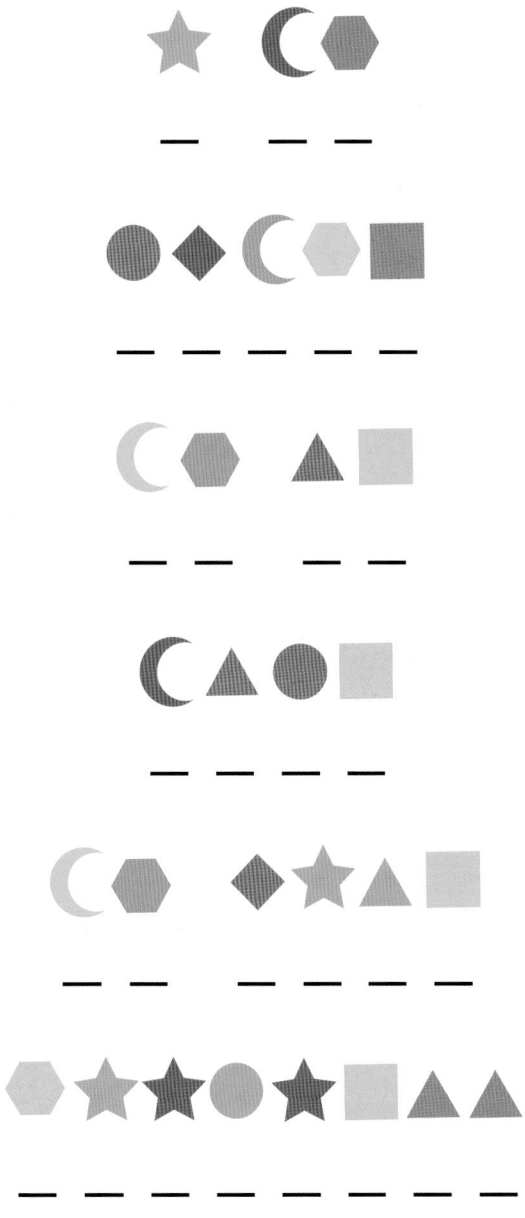

WHAT CARING JOB SHOULD I DO?

Try this fun quiz to see how you could use your kindness to do good in the world! What caring role would be perfect for you?

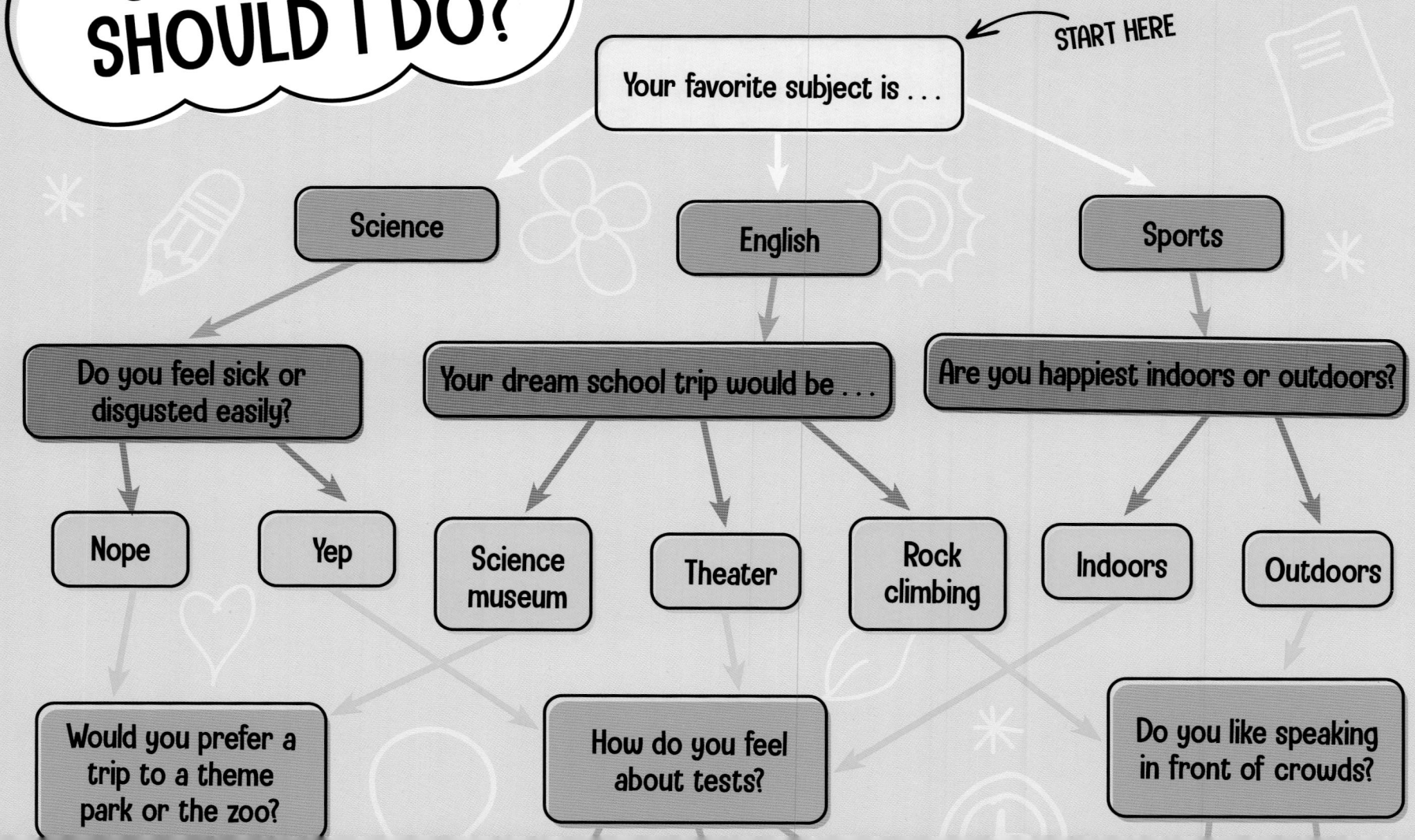

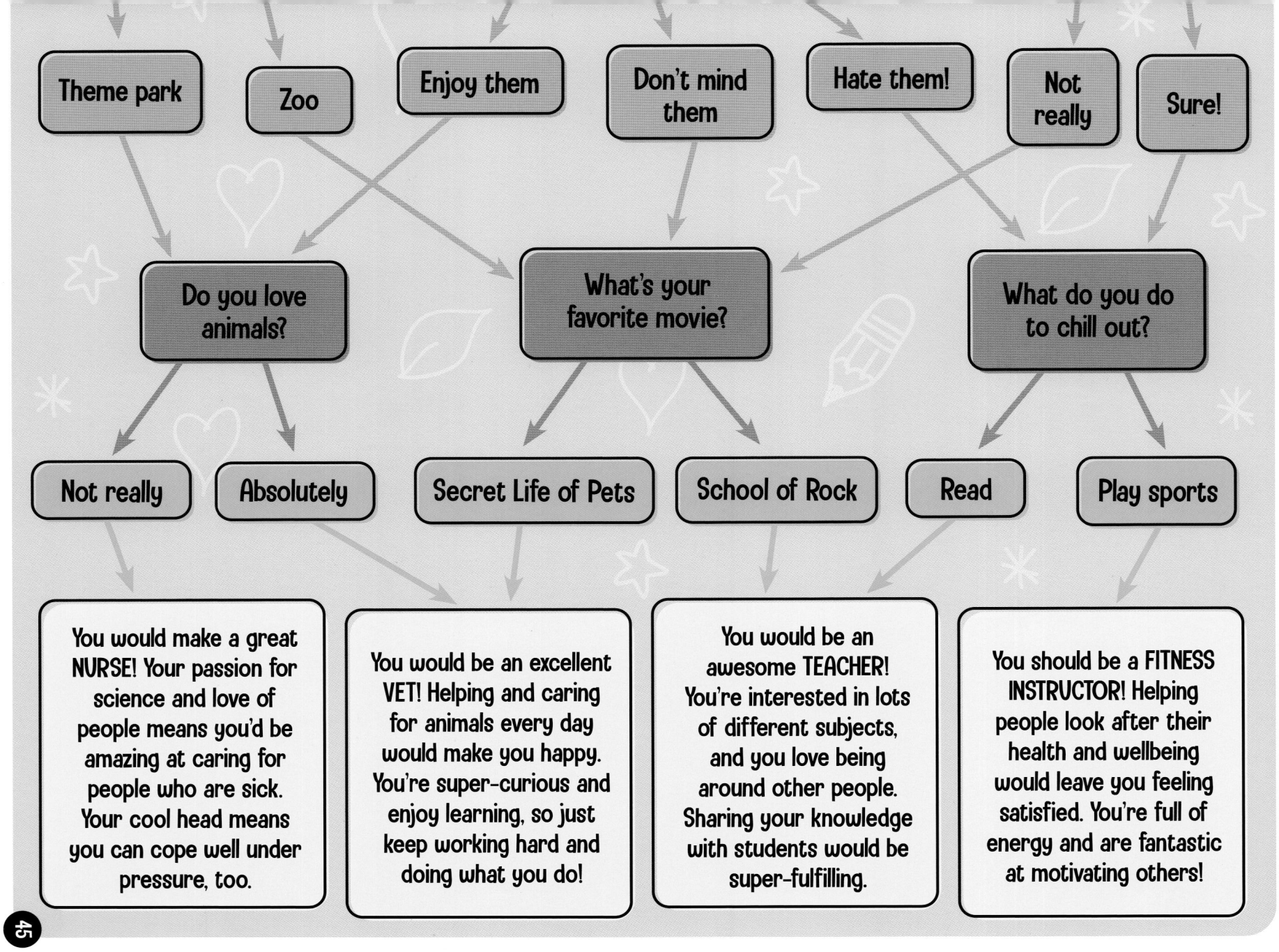
Theme park
Zoo
Enjoy them
Don't mind them
Hate them!
Not really
Sure!
Do you love animals?
What's your favorite movie?
What do you do to chill out?
Not really
Absolutely
Secret Life of Pets
School of Rock
Read
Play sports
You would make a great NURSE! Your passion for science and love of people means you'd be amazing at caring for people who are sick. Your cool head means you can cope well under pressure, too.
You would be an excellent VET! Helping and caring for animals every day would make you happy. You're super-curious and enjoy learning, so just keep working hard and doing what you do!
You would be an awesome TEACHER! You're interested in lots of different subjects, and you love being around other people. Sharing your knowledge with students would be super-fulfilling.
You should be a FITNESS INSTRUCTOR! Helping people look after their health and wellbeing would leave you feeling satisfied. You're full of energy and are fantastic at motivating others!

COLOR ME KIND

Kind Ninja and Caring Ninja noticed that Shy Ninja had nobody to play with, so they invited Shy Ninja to play with them!

ALL SCRAMBLED UP!
Anxious Ninja is writing party invitations, but all of the ninja names are mixed up! Can you unscramble them to reveal the right names?
It's really kind of you to help me!
SLINETING L _ _ _ _ _ _ _ _ _
YSH _ _ _
FELLHUP H _ _ _ _ _ _ _
NARGY _ _ _ _ _
OUTIMABIS A _ _ _ _ _ _ _ _ _
DINK _ _ _ _

LET'S SKETCH

Drawing and coloring is a fun way to unwind—and it's a great way to practice self-care. Draw Kind Ninja using the grid to help you.

Finding a peaceful place to sit and create something is one of the ways I am kind to myself.

A GOOD FRIEND IS . . .

Color in the top 10 qualities you look for in a friend. There are no right or wrong answers—it's up to YOU!

Honest

Happy

Kind

Organized

Silly

Caring

A good listener

Good at video games

Respectful

Funny

Supportive

Protective

Encouraging

Accepting

Be kind to yourself! Spend time with friends who bring out the best in you.

Clever

Athletic

Understanding

Individual

A bookworm

Adventurous

THINK ABOUT TWO FRIENDS AND WRITE DOWN THREE OF THEIR BEST TRAITS IN THESE BOXES.

NAME: .....

BEST QUALITIES:

1. .....

.....

2. .....

.....

3. .....

.....

NAME: .....

BEST QUALITIES:

1. .....

.....

2. .....

.....

3. .....

.....

How did this activity make YOU feel?

Add a thumbs up or a thumbs down sticker here.

CHEERFUL MESSAGE

Random acts of kindness remind people that they are loved and special. Draw pictures or write a thoughtful message in the strings of triangular flags to cheer someone up, then color them in!

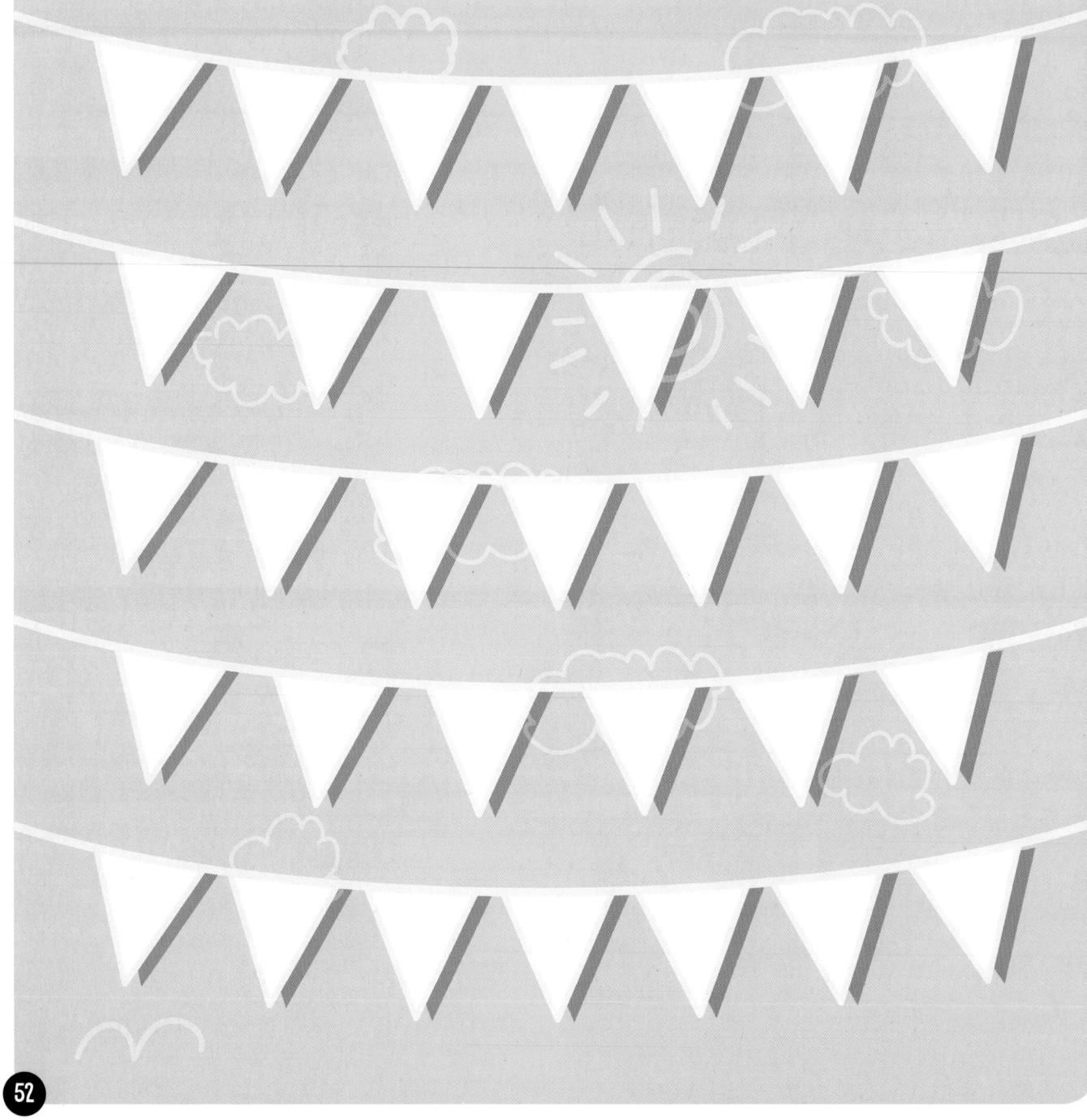

MY KINDNESS PLEDGE

Writing a pledge is like making a promise to yourself. Use this page to jot down a list of all the ways you want to be kind every day.

IDEAS
ENCOURAGE OTHERS, BE RESPECTFUL, SHARE MY THINGS, HELP MY NEIGHBOR.

My pledges . . .

Write your pledges on a piece of paper and read them every day as a reminder to be kind.

BE KIND

It can be hard to see someone you care about going through a tough time. Arm yourself with these ideas from Kind Ninja to help give them support! As you try each idea, check it off or put a star sticker next to it!

Say something positive about them

Watch a funny TV show or movie together

Lend them your favorite book

Remind them of a funny memory you share

Tell them that they can always talk to you

Do something silly to make them laugh

Suggest they talk to a trusted grownup

Check each one when you have tried it.

Listen to their worries

Ask them to join in whatever activity you are doing

Invite them to your house after school

Make a card for them

Offer to sit together at lunchtime

Share your snack with them

Tell them your favorite joke

Surprise them with something delicious

Do something creative together, like making a scrapbook or drawing

Include them in your games during recess

Encourage them to talk to you about what's worrying them

Introduce them to your friends

LOST LUNCH

Disappointed Ninja forgot to bring lunch to school today. Luckily, Sharing Ninja has offered to share. Can you figure out which lunch is the mirror image of the big picture? Check the right answer.

A

B

C

I have plenty for both of us.

Thanks so much!

SPREAD THE WORD

Kindness can become your secret weapon against cruelty in the world. Design a poster with a message about kindness! Use pictures, stickers, symbols, words, or poetry—it's up to you!

THINK ABOUT WHERE YOU WOULD HANG YOUR POSTER SO THAT LOTS OF PEOPLE WOULD SEE IT!

Ninja Life Hacks

KINDNESS BANQUET
Good food brings people together! Grab your colored pencils and get doodling to fill this table with tasty treats for everyone to share.
I was feeling super hangry, but not anymore!

LET'S SKATE
These ninjas were having fun skating at the park until Helpful Ninja fell. Follow the tangled lines to see which ninja will reach Helpful Ninja first.
Kind Ninja
Brave Ninja
Love Ninja
Focused Ninja
Thank you for helping me.

CELEBRATE DIFFERENCE

If everybody was the same, the world wouldn't be very interesting! Embracing diversity is about being kind and learning from one another.

USE THE NUMBERS IN THE COLOR KEY TO HELP YOU COMPLETE THIS PICTURE.

COLOR KEY

1	3	5	7
2	4	6	8

No matter our differences, we should always be kind to others.

SHOW SUPPORT

These ninja friends are cheering Anxious Ninja on to the finish line of the race. Complete this puzzle by putting the pieces in the right place.

ACTS OF KINDNESS

Read each idea carefully and sort them into two categories! Color the kind acts in yellow and the unkind acts in blue.

KIND

UNKIND

Share your snack

Laugh at someone's mistake

Write a letter to a grandparent or relative

Copy someone's schoolwork

Invite a friend to your house

Write a poem for a special person

Leave one person out in a game

Stand up for someone who is sad

Cut in line

Ignore someone

Bring someone a souvenir from your vacation

Say mean things behind a friend's back

Run an errand

Offer to help a friend with homework
Ask someone on their own to join in
Yell at someone
Talk over someone when they speak
Bake cookies to share
Eat someone's snack without asking
Hold the door open for someone
Leave a nice note in your friend's backpack
Help carry someone's shopping bags
Hug someone
Blame others for your mistake
Compliment someone
Which ideas will you try with your friends?
Random acts of kindness can make you feel good, too!

MIX UP

Unscramble the letters below to reveal the hidden words! Here's a clue: Each word relates to the theme of kindness.

1. T E N G L E

2. L U P H E L F

3. F A C E T I F O N A T E

4. R A C I N G

5. R U G S E N E O

I'm Stressed Ninja.
When people show me kindness, it helps me feel calm.

COME TOGETHER

Kindness is contagious! It helps you to make friends and feel happier! Use your favorite colors to finish this picture.

How did this activity make YOU feel?

Add a thumbs up or a thumbs down sticker here.

WHAT KIND OF FRIEND ARE YOU?

Try this fun quiz to discover what type of friend you are! Don't forget to keep track of your answers.

1. On the weekend, I'm most likely to be . . .
   a. Chilling at home with my best friend
   b. Organizing the next social event
   c. Out and about with friends
   d. Doing something with my family

2. If there's a bake sale at your school, what do you do?
   a. Buy a cupcake to surprise my bestie
   b. Help organize what everyone is making so there is a good variety
   c. Get there early so I have the pick of the best food
   d. Spend my entire allowance on treats

3. Pick an activity you would like to do most!
   a. Going on a hike
   b. Exploring a new city
   c. Riding my bike
   d. Taking an art class

4. When it comes to homework, I . . .
   a. Take my time to get it done well
   b. Always complete it early
   c. Put it off for as long as possible
   d. Offer to help others

5. My favorite subject at school is . . .
   a. English
   b. Math
   c. Science
   d. Art

6. When I pack for a vacation, I . . .
   a. Keep things simple
   b. Write a list
   c. Take as much as possible
   d. Pack light

7. My dream vacation would be . . .
   a. A peaceful beach
   b. A sightseeing city tour
   c. A safari
   d. A family vacation to our favorite place

8. My bedroom is . . .

a. My calm and happy place
b. Super neat and tidy
c. Always being switched up and painted new colors depending on the latest trends
d. The same as it's always been since I was little

9. When there is a big change in my life, I feel . . .

a. Cool as a cucumber
b. Prepared
c. Excited
d. Nervous

10. If I'm worried about something, I . . .

a. Mostly keep it to myself or talk to my family
b. Find a person who can help me with the specific issue
c. Talk to everyone
d. Talk to one friend I can trust

11. In class, I'm the one that . . .

a. Works quietly to get things done
b. Always has my hand up asking lots of questions
c. Volunteers to read out loud or do presentations
d. Offers to help others if they don't understand

12. My favorite animals are . . .

a. Dolphins
b. Meerkats
c. Cats
d. Dogs

Mostly As

You are the best listener. You put other people's needs before your own, and you love being there for friends when they need you. What's more, you are so thoughtful and always generous with your time. Just remember to look after yourself—you're important, too!

Mostly Bs

You are the organizer! Whether it's bake sales, parties, or games on the playground, it's you who makes sure everybody's days are packed with fun. Your pals know they can turn to you if they missed what homework was given or forgot their lunch—you always have it covered.

Mostly Cs

You are the leader. You know what you want, and you're not afraid to be different or stand out in the crowd. Your friends admire your confidence, and they tend to follow your lead. The best thing is that you make those around you feel awesome, too!

Mostly Ds

You are loyal. Your besties know that when you make a promise, you'll keep it. Everyone knows they can trust and rely on you, because you've always got their back. Family means everything to you, so a fun trip with them is just as exciting as hanging with your pals.

SHOW COMPASSION

Be gentle, show kindness, and treat all living things with respect. Connect the dots to see Compassionate Ninja taking care of this little dog.

DON'T FORGET TO COLOR IN YOUR PICTURE.

MAKE A KINDNESS FLOWER

Think of some different ways that you can be kind and write them in the petals. Draw a picture of yourself or write your name in the center and then color it in.

WHY NOT DRAW AND COLOR A KINDNESS FLOWER TO PUT ON YOUR BEDROOM WALL?

30-DAY KINDNESS CHALLENGE

Ready to take on Kind Ninja's challenge? Choose one challenge every day and color in the stars as you try each one!

1 ☆ Help out with chores at home	2 ☆ Talk to someone about a favorite memory you share with them	3 ☆ Help set the table for dinner	4 ☆ Say thank you to your teacher	5 ☆ Take a bubble bath
6 ☆ Lend something to somebody	7 ☆ Give someone a hug	8 ☆ Write down three things that you did well today	9 ☆ Pick up trash around your neighborhood	10 ☆ Share toys with a sibling or friend
11 ☆ Write a thank you letter	12 ☆ Smile at someone who looks sad	13 ☆ Remember to say please and thank you at home	14 ☆ Tell your sibling something you love about them	15 ☆ Encourage a classmate

16 ☆ Say hi to the new person	17 ☆ Offer to help your teacher	18 ☆ Donate a toy you no longer use	19 ☆ Make someone laugh with your best joke	20 ☆ Treat yourself to doing your favorite thing
21 ☆ Draw a picture and give it to a friend	22 ☆ Help someone make new friends	23 ☆ Look in the mirror and say something kind to yourself	24 ☆ Wait for a friend who can't keep up	25 ☆ Make a card for a family member and put it on their pillow to surprise them
26 ☆ Clean up your room before you're asked to	27 ☆ Help someone with their homework	28 ☆ Ask someone how they are feeling	29 ☆ Listen to someone's worries	30 ☆ Make a card for one of your neighbors

ASK YOUR FAMILY AND FRIENDS TO TAKE ON THE CHALLENGE, TOO!

FOUR WAYS

There are four ninjas on this page, and they all need a little kindness! Write or draw a different act of kindness to cheer up each ninja.

Worry Ninja

Sad Ninja

Lonely Ninja

Nervous Ninja

IDEAS!
BAKE COOKIES, MAKE A CARD, GIVE THEM A HUG, OR GET LOTS OF FRIENDS TOGETHER.

LET'S PLAY SQUARES

Find a friend to play a game of squares. Take turns connecting two dots with a line. If a player draws a line that completes a box, they write their initials in the square. The player with the most initialed squares at the end, wins!

TAKE THE TROPHY

Write down three things about you that make you awesome, then color in the trophy using your favorite colors.

How did this activity make YOU feel?

Add a thumbs up or a thumbs down sticker here.

KINDNESS COUNTS

There are lots of kind people out there doing wonderful things. Use this page to jot down any acts of kindness that you see going on around you or in the news—big or small!

YOU MAY NOTICE SOMEONE HELP A STRANGER CROSS THE ROAD, CHECK ON AN ELDERLY NEIGHBOR, OR SURPRISE SOMEONE WITH A CAKE. YOU MAY SPOT SOMEONE DONATING TO A FOOD BANK OR SAYING GOOD MORNING TO A BUS DRIVER.

How did this activity make YOU feel?
Add a thumbs up or a thumbs down sticker here.

KIND WORDS

Kind Ninja and Compassionate Ninja have written the word "KINDNESS" on the board. Can you think of a word or phrase about kindness that starts with each letter? Write them in the blank spaces. We started one for you.

K .....

I .....

N .....

D .....

N ever leave anybody out .....

E .....

S .....

S .....

Kind words are powerful words!

BE INCLUSIVE

Being inclusive means including everyone and sticking together! Color in these ninjas to finish the picture.

Answers:

PAGE 10: WHAT COMES NEXT?

A. B. C. D.

PAGE 11: MATCH UP–E AND G MATCH.

PAGE 16: MY KIND OF TREAT

PAGES 18–19: SPREAD KINDNESS

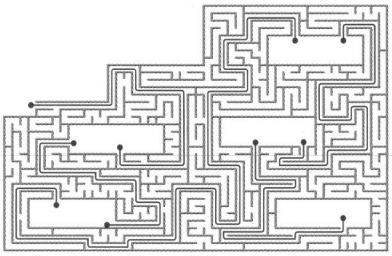

PAGE 20: WORD SEARCH

A	T	H	O	U	G	H	T	F	U	L	R	U	Y	F
G	U	A	C	O	Y	H	O	P	I	Q	Z	F	N	K
P	A	R	F	C	P	N	R	C	X	Z	O	B	K	J
A	E	N	F	A	C	L	U	O	M	Y	M	P	I	D
T	W	D	Q	R	O	E	U	M	S	A	H	F	N	A
I	S	Z	U	I	I	E	X	P	O	H	E	S	D	E
E	Y	P	P	N	A	H	G	A	B	N	L	A	O	F
N	H	G	C	G	C	E	P	S	T	Q	P	Y	H	V
C	F	C	E	X	D	M	U	S	H	L	F	B	G	Y
E	T	I	L	H	X	N	L	I	S	E	U	B	D	I
A	X	O	E	A	T	Y	I	O	H	T	L	K	Y	Z
R	H	U	G	T	X	L	H	N	Q	K	C	M	S	Q
O	T	Z	V	L	O	V	E	B	T	I	O	N	F	U
S	E	L	F	N	E	S	S	S	C	C	M	K	B	L
E	A	M	N	I	D	L	R	Y	E	Q	Y	S	N	M

PAGES 26–27: SPOT THE DIFFERENCE

PAGE 28: SHARING IS CARING–EACH NINJA GETS TWO DONUTS.

PAGE 29: MIX UP–F, C, D, B, A, E

PAGE 33: SIZE SORTING–A. 10, B. 8, C. 1, D. 7, E. 2, F. 6, G. 5, H. 3, I. 4, J. 9

PAGE 34–35: STICK TOGETHER

PAGE 36: SUDOKU

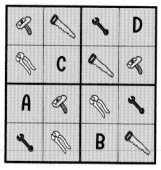

PAGE 38: TO THE PARK

PAGE 39: WHICH NINJA?

PAGES 40–41: KINDNESS AT PLAY

4 4 5 2 5 3 4 3 2 2

PAGES 43: CRACK THE CODE–
I AM LUCKY TO BE ABLE TO GIVE KINDNESS

PAGE 46: COLOR ME KIND

PAGE 47: SCRAMBLED–
1. LISTENING NINJA, 2. SHY NINJA, 3. HELPFUL NINJA, 4. ANGRY NINJA, 5. AMBITIOUS NINJA, 6. KIND NINJA

PAGE 56: LOST LUNCH–C

PAGE 59: LET'S SKATE

PAGE 60: CELEBRATE DIFFERENCE

PAGE 61: SHOW SUPPORT

PAGE 64: MIX UP–
1. GENTLE, 2. HELPFUL, 3. AFFECTIONATE, 4. CARING, 5. GENEROUS

PAGE 68: SHOW COMPASSION